Run, jump, climb and crawl

The essential training guide for obstacle racing enthusiasts, or how to get fit, stay safe and prepare for the toughest mud runs on the planet

By

Jacob Salt-Berrymen

Discover more books and ebooks of interest to you and find out about the range of work we do at the forefront of health, fitness and wellbeing.

www.ymcaed.org.uk

Published by Central YMCA Trading Ltd (trading as YMCAed). Registered Company No. 3667206.

Copyright © Central YMCA Trading Ltd 2013
Cover photo courtesy of 'Mud Runner; Nothing Tougher' www.mudrunner.co.uk
All rights reserved. No part of this publication may be reproduced, stored in a retrieval system, or transmitted, in any form or by any means, without the prior permission of the publisher.

YMCAed
Central YMCA Trading Ltd
112 Great Russell Street
London
WC1B 3NQ

www.ymcaed.org.uk

ISBN: 1490340556
ISBN-13: 978-1490340555

This book is presented solely for educational and entertainment purposes. The author and publisher are not offering it as legal, medical, or other professional services advice. While best efforts have been used in preparing this book, the author and publisher make no representations or warranties of any kind and assume no liabilities of any kind with respect to the accuracy or completeness of the contents and specifically disclaim any implied warranties of merchantability or fitness of use for a particular purpose. Neither the publisher nor the individual author(s) shall be liable for any physical, psychological, emotional, financial, or commercial damages, including, but not limited to, special, incidental, consequential or other damages, resulting from the information or programs contained herein. Every person is different and the information, advice and programs contained herein may not be suitable for your situation. Exercise is not without its risks and, as such, we would strongly advise that you consult with your healthcare professional before beginning any programme of exercise, especially if you have, or suspect you may have, any injuries or illnesses, are currently pregnant or have recently given birth. The advice, information and guidance given in Central YMCA Guides is in no way intended as a substitute for medical consultation. As with any form of exercise, you should stop immediately if you feel faint, dizzy or have physical discomfort or pain or any other contra indication, and consult a physician.

Central YMCA is the world's founding YMCA. Established in 1844 in Central London, it was the first YMCA to open its doors and, in so doing, launched a movement that has now grown to become the world's biggest youth organisation. Today, Central YMCA is the UK's leading health, fitness and wellbeing charity, committed to helping people from all walks of life – and specifically the young and those with a specific need – to live happier, healthier and more fulfilled lives.

TABLE OF CONTENTS

ABOUT THE AUTHOR vii

ACKNOWLEDGEMENTS 9

INTRODUCTION 11

1 CHOOSING YOUR RACE 13

2 DEMANDS OF OBSTACLE RACING 17

3 FUEL YOUR FIRE 21

4 WEAR IT WITH PRIDE 27

5 WORKING UP A SWEAT 33

6 KNOW YOUR ENEMY 35

7 RACE TACTICS 43

8 FAIL TO PREPARE, PREPARE TO FAIL 47

9 RACE DAY 49

10 ZERO TO HERO IN 12 WEEKS TRAINING PLAN 53

11 THE WORKOUTS 61

12 RUNNING FOR CHARITY FAQ 69

BIBLIOGRAPHY 73

ALSO OUT NOW 75

THE CENTRAL YMCA GUIDE SERIES 77

ABOUT THE AUTHOR

Hello, and thanks for buying this book. By doing so I am going to guess that you have a curious mind and a passing interest in obstacle racing, are preparing for your first ever event, or have, like me, become a mud-loving, obstacle racing addict.

Whatever your reason for buying this book, I hope you enjoy reading it as much as I have enjoyed writing it.

To give you a bit of background, I'm a philosophy graduate of the University of Greenwich in London, a personal trainer, regular triathlete and enthusiastic obstacle racer.

I'm also a Fitness Tutor for YMCA Fitness Industry Training – an operation of Central YMCA, the UK's leading activity for health charity – and I specialise in outdoor fitness, suspension training, and anatomy and physiology, all of which have helped me to understand the unique training requirements of obstacle racing and the challenges it presents to runners.

This book therefore sets out to ensure that you, dear reader, are fully prepared for the obstacle race that lies ahead of you, complete with all its crawling, climbing, jumping, dodging and electrifying (!) obstacles.

Although there is no record of his ever having jumped through fire or swum through icy water, Benjamin Franklin once said that 'by failing to prepare, you are preparing to fail'.

So, prepare to read on if you want to complete, and survive, your next obstacle race.

See you in the mud,

Jacob

Central YMCA Health and Fitness Guides

ACKNOWLEDGEMENTS

Thank you to all the people I have had the privilege of racing with – you know who you are.

Thank you to all the mysterious mud-clad figures who have picked me up and spurred me on during some of the toughest events.

Finally, thank you to my close friends and family who have made this book possible.

Central YMCA Health and Fitness Guides

INTRODUCTION

Congratulations, by deciding to buy this book you've taken your first step, or leap, towards the finish line of what may well be your first obstacle race.

The following pages will cover everything you need to know to get you from your sofa to the finishing line, including what types of races to choose, what demands they will place on your fitness and your body, what obstacles you are likely to face and, vitally, how you can train for them.

However, let's begin with the basics...

WHAT ARE OBSTACLE RACES?

In its simplest form an obstacle race involves running from one point to another, between which you must complete a number of physical or psychological challenges designed to hinder your progress.

Some races will rely purely on terrain to provide obstacles – such as hills, streams, rocks and plenty of mud – while others will employ manmade obstacles such as vast climbing frames, seemingly impossible walls and balance beams suspended above the floor. In other words, think giant army assault courses.

This book is aimed at preparing you for events that are essentially a hybrid between these two types of race; in the coming pages we'll look at what obstacles you might expect to find during your race and the logistical considerations you should make before entering and starting it.

WHY ARE THESE RACES SO POPULAR?

Obstacle racing can be dated back to the early 1990s with races such as Tough Guy (England) and Camp Pendleton Mud Run (USA) in which competitors battled through courses of obstacles and mud with the sole intent of completing the run, rather than setting the course record.

These types of races have grown in popularity over the years to the point where they are selling out with over 5,000 competitors entering each event. This upsurge in popularity can be put down to the fact that these races offer a unique challenge to participants: they are a novelty, require a low skill level and do not require competitors to invest in expensive kit (unlike events such as triathlons). These races also harbour a much friendlier, even party-like atmosphere where the emphasis is placed on having a great time and getting a bit mucky, instead of pounding pavements for miles on end.

So, now that we've got the basics sussed, let's get training.

1

CHOOSING YOUR RACE

WHAT RACES ARE AVAILABLE?

Wild races
These races will be run more or less completely off-road. So, not only will you have obstacles to tackle, but you'll also have to contend with the local geography; streams, muddy bogs, big hills and rock strewn descents all likely to be included.

Wild races are usually a short drive away from the city, which can make them fairly inaccessible if you don't have a car or some kind person to drive you there. It's also worth noting that the course and obstacles will often take more of a beating from the weather than those that feature in an urban race. For example, if you are running through woodland or farm land in an area that has recently seen heavy rainfall, then the mud on the course will give you a 100% naturally occurring extra challenge.

Urban races
These races are run mainly through the streets of a major city, taking in obstacles along the way. These will often make use of large parks or open spaces within the city to offer a variety of terrain. Urban races will also include industrial obstacles to give an authentic urban feel. Expect hollowed out cars to crawl through, abandoned warehouses turned into assault

courses and skips filled with freezing water or mud (an essential element of any obstacle race).

Obstacle dense races

The number of obstacles over the length of a course can vary greatly from race to race. However, you will be able to get a good feel for the obstacle density of the race you have in mind by visiting the race website and watching videos of previous races – almost always available on YouTube.

Some races, for example, will only have one or two obstacles per kilometre over, say, a 10km course. Such races will require you to be able to run consistently for longer periods of time, perhaps 5-15 minutes before you get to an obstacle. Points to bear in mind include:

- *Spread:* Because of the distance between obstacles the field of competitors inevitably spreads out more; this makes it is easier to find your own space within these races – see the *Race tactics* section.
- *Training:* If your race is very heavy on running, replicate this in your training by running for longer distances broken up with two or three exercises from the *Know your enemy* section.

Other races may be more densely populated with obstacles – the most I have seen in one race totalled a staggering 30 over a 5km lap. For these kinds of races there is less emphasis on running long distances between obstacles and much more focus on the climbing, jumping and crawling element of obstacle racing.

Naturally, due to the large number of obstacles there is a higher probability of bunching at obstacles – see the *Race tactics* section.

Remember: If your race is obstacle dense, replicate this during your training; run for two minutes followed by three, four or five exercises from the *Know your enemy* section.

Single loop vs. multiple loop

Some races will involve a single loop covering the whole distance of the race, while others may allow you to choose the distance you want to race based on the number of loops of the same course that you wish to run. If the latter is the situation, you will need to specify the number of loops (from the organiser's pre-determined number) you are planning to race when you book your place, as there will usually be a different price depending on the number of loops you will run.

If you are running a looped race it will take a great deal of mental strength to tackle the same obstacles loop after loop. You will also find that the obstacles will become harder to tackle as more and more competitors cross over, under or through them. If on the day, however, you realise that you have bitten off more than you can chew you can always head for the finish line instead of turning the corner for that extra lap. You will see this happen more frequently in races where the weather is bad and competitors simply want to finish in order to get warm and dry!

Team races
Some races require you to run as part of a team of between two and five people. Team races will include obstacles for which you will need more than one person to conquer – these could include climbing challenges, kayaking challenges or even three legged races! Some races will specify that teams must be mixed, so check this out on the race website.

Remember: If you are running as a team it is useful to train together so you can assess each other's strengths and weaknesses and come up with support strategies for race day.

The extreme factor
Lots of the more commercial events will market themselves along the lines of being the 'Toughest Ever Challenge' – and most of them will have good reason to do so.

As obstacle racing has grown in popularity the obstacles themselves have become more and more extreme (although not in every race) to keep people coming back for more. Most races that class themselves as extreme will employ obstacles deliberately designed to cause dread or inflict pain upon participants; crawling through pitch black tunnels, being submerged in ice cold water, jumping through flames or being electrocuted (yes, electrocuted!) are all commonly occurring obstacles in the more extreme races.

The extreme factor can also extend to distance or time spent running in races. There are races as long as or longer than a marathon and littered with obstacles throughout, as if a marathon wasn't hard enough already! Similarly, there are races that take place through the night from 6 to 12 to even 24 hours in length.

Obstacle racing is about challenging yourself, and even though you may get more people to sponsor you or more bragging rights for running 'The Most

Extreme Race Ever Created', it is important to consider what you actually want to get out of it and how much you are willing to go through.

Other considerations

Location, accommodation and travel
Can you get there and back in a day or do you need to book overnight accommodation? Remember that you will want to arrive at the race well in advance of your start time for your piece of mind and you may want to celebrate afterwards without having to drive home.

If you are booking a hotel and running as a group, make sure you get your accommodation booked nice and early. There's nothing more infuriating than being the only one of your team-mates in a different hotel!

Spectators
It is lovely if friends and family come to watch you race and cheer you on from the side lines, because a friendly face can be a welcome sight when you stagger across the finish line. Spectators can also perform vital duties during the race such as being your (or your team's) official photographer and pit crew. Pit crew duties, in my experience, mainly involve feeding you jelly babies at strategic intervals during the race.

There will usually be specific vantage points where your friends and family can watch you and cheer you on. Although if the weather is poor you might find them in the beer tent hiding from the rain or back in the car keeping warm.

2

DEMANDS OF OBSTACLE RACING

If you thought you were fit, think again. Obstacle racing will challenge all aspects of your fitness. Everyone will have strengths and weaknesses across the different components of fitness highlighted below, so try to identify yours and use the techniques that follow to increase your performance in each area.

CARDIOVASCULAR

What is it?
Cardiovascular fitness is your body's ability to work, rhythmically, at a moderate to high intensity over an extended period of time.

Examples of use during a typical race:

- The main challenge for your cardiovascular (CV) system – the main energy system that you will use throughout the race – will come from running over, through, around and between obstacles. By training your CV system you will be able to work at higher intensities for longer periods of time. This translates to being able to run your race harder and therefore faster than all your mates.

- Also, by having a strong CV system your recovery time will be lower, and this translates to being able to get your breath back (recover) faster after you have completed a sprint or an obstacle.
- Areas in this book's training plan (see *Zero to hero in 12 weeks*) which target this system:
    - All of the running done during the programme will increase your CV fitness.
    - All the circuit sessions where you are performing exercises back to back with minimal rest.

MUSCULAR STRENGTH

What is it?

Muscular strength is your ability to produce a maximal force for a low number of repetitions, between one and six. Olympic power-lifting is a great example of pure muscular strength.

Examples of use during a typical race:

- The main challenges for muscular strength will come from obstacles which involve single explosive movements. For example, jumping to clear a high hurdle or pulling yourself over a giant wall (in one move).
- By having stronger muscles you will be able to exert more force per single maximal contraction. This translates to being able to jump higher or further, or pull yourself over obstacles at a faster rate. If you have developed your muscles to exert a high maximal force during your training you may find that for certain obstacles they will not have to contract maximally to conquer them – this means obstacles will feel easier.
- Other benefits include stronger ligaments and tendons which will aid joint stability and can lower your risk of injury.
- Areas in this book's training plan (see *Zero to hero in 12 weeks*) which target this system:
    - Weeks 5-6 specifically work on muscular strength.
    - Any sessions where you are completing between 1 and 6 repetitions and are unable to complete any more due to fatigue.

MUSCULAR FITNESS/ENDURANCE

What is it?
Muscular fitness/endurance refers to the ability of your muscles to contract sub-maximally for a higher number of repetitions; 8-12 for fitness and 12-30 for endurance.

Examples of use during a typical race:

- The challenges for your muscular endurance will come from obstacles requiring you to perform a number of resisted moves or contractions in a short space of time, some examples might include pulling your legs through or out of a mud pit, climbing a cargo net or pulling yourself up a slope using a rope.
- By training for muscular endurance you will be able to exert higher sub-maximal contractions over a longer period of time. This translates to you being able to traverse obstacles faster and will make them feel as though they are easier.
- Areas in this book's training plan (see *Zero to hero in 12 weeks*) which target this system:
  - This component will be targeted by all sessions where the exercises are performed with high repetitions.

MENTAL STRENGTH

What is it?
Mental strength or mental toughness is hard to define; it is intangible and unquantifiable. There are no set exercises or repetition ranges for the mind. Mental strength is more about your resolve and your ability to keep going and keep fighting when you feel ready to give up.

Examples of use during a typical race:

- Mental toughness can come into play when dealing with obstacles which take you high off the ground; fear of the height/fear of falling can grip people and root them to the spot.
- Lapped races require a good deal of mental toughness – most lapped races take you within metres of the finish line before you have to head in the other direction to complete your remaining laps, something that can be hard to take when you're tired and hungry.

- It can also be as simple as exhaustion. Indeed, there may be points during the race where it becomes so intense, or you feel so tired, that you feel as if you will not be able to complete it.
- You can help to boost your mental toughness or resolve by putting yourself into similar positions before the race. By training at high intensities (which you will be doing by the end of the 12-week plan) in similar conditions will get your mind used to functioning under that kind of pressure. Further to this, if you know that you will encounter obstacles that you will struggle with – e.g. being a long way off the floor – then slowly build yourself up to dealing with the issue during your training runs. With the height example, for instance, you could get used to climbing up onto ledges and getting back down again, starting small and working up gradually. It will also be helpful to have people with you when you decide to do this; they can give you encouragement or save you if you really do freeze.
- Other mental preparation should include visualisation. This is where you take time to imagine (mentally rehearse) yourself running the course and taking on the obstacles with no hesitation or hindrance. By doing this you will begin to feel comfortable with what you will come up against in the race and, on the day, you should be able to tap into or step into those feelings to traverse and scale all the obstacles in exactly the way you had practised in both your physical and mental rehearsals. And, if you think visualisation is all a bit naff, remember that some of the greatest sports men and women in the world use it as a training tool. Formula One drivers, for instance, are coached on visualisation as a method of preparing for the perfect qualifying lap.
- Areas in this book's training plan (see *Zero to hero in 12 weeks*) which target this system:
  - o By training hard in all conditions you will prepare your mind to perform well under these conditions.
  - o There is no set time suggested for visualisations – so set yourself some time to enjoy a good daydream!

3

FUEL YOUR FIRE

HOW MUCH SHOULD YOU BE EATING?

To determine how many calories you should be consuming per day throughout the build up to your race, you need to work out your basal metabolic rate (BMR) and multiply this figure by your current activity levels.

Your BMR is the number of calories your body needs to keep all your basic functions ticking over throughout the day; heart beating, breathing in and out etc. This does not include moving around, going to and from work and it definitely does not include exercise.

There are many ways to work out your BMR, the quick method is as follows:

- Men – 24kcal per 1.0kg body weight
- Women – 22kcal per 1.0kg body weight

Example: 80kg male = 80 x 24 = 1,920kcal
(Bean, 2002)

Another way of working out your BMR is the Harris Benedict method (*http://www.bmi-calculator.net/bmr-calculator/harris-benedict-equation / ymcaed.org.uk/hbe*). This does take slightly longer but is more accurate as it takes into account two variables which the above method does not, namely height and age.

Men

66 + (13.7 x weight in kg) + (5 x height in cm) – (6.8 x age)

Women

665 + (9.6 x weight in kg) + (1.8 x height in cm) – (4.7 x age)

Example: 80kg male who is 182cm and 25 years old =
66 + (13.7 x 80) + (5 x 182) – (6.8 x 25) = 2,222kcal
*(http://www.bmi-calculator.net/bmr-calculator/bmr-formula.php /
ymcaed.org.uk/bmr)*
Once you have established your BMR you need to multiply this number with how active you are on a day to day basis:

- Sedentary (little to no activity) x 1.2
- Lightly active (light activity or sport 1-3 times per week) x 1.375
- Moderately active (moderate intensity activity or sport 3-5 times per week) x 1.55
- Very active (hard activity or sports 6-7 times per week) x 1.75
- Extremely active (physical job and also training hard more than once per day) x 1.9

*(http://www.bmi-calculator.net/bmr-calculator/harris-benedict-equation /
ymcaed.org.uk/hbe)*

Example: Our 80kg man who is moderately active would need 2,222 x 1.55
= 3,333kcal

So, now that you have a gauge of how much you should be eating, make sure you get the necessary calories through good sources and in the right balance. You could use the FSA food plate as a guide to your meals *(http://www.food.gov.uk)*. Alternatively, check out The Need to Know Guide to Nutrition for Exercise from Central YMCA Guides *(ymcaed.org.uk/gnhe)* for a complete guide to eating and drinking the right foods to meet your exercise needs and goals.

FUELLING YOUR TRAINING AND RACE

When it comes to training and racing it is vital that you make sure you never run on empty. By not having enough food for your body to use as fuel you will fatigue faster, which will result in decreased performance in both your workouts and your races.

When you run on empty your body is not encouraged to use more of its fat stores, instead it will use your own muscle fibres for fuel as these are easier to access. Also, by not taking in enough fuel you are running the risk of nausea, dizziness and fainting, which can all result from a subsequent dip in blood sugar levels.

So, to ensure your body is adequately fuelled for the challenges ahead, you should eat something two to four hours before you train or race. These foods should rank low down the glycaemic index (GI) scale as this will ensure a stable level of blood sugar.

Glycaemic index - *"The glycemic index (GI) is a ranking of carbohydrates on a scale from 0 to 100 according to the extent to which they raise blood sugar levels after eating. Foods with a high GI are those which are rapidly digested and absorbed and result in marked fluctuations in blood sugar levels. Low-GI foods, by virtue of their slow digestion and absorption, produce gradual rises in blood sugar and insulin levels, and have proven benefits for health." (http://www.glycemicindex.com/about.php) / ymcaed.org.uk/gi)*

Low-GI examples include:
- Jacket potato with tuna or beans or chicken
- Porridge made with milk
- Rice or noodles with chicken and vegetable stir-fry
- Pasta in tomato sauce with vegetables

You may find that you need a pre-workout snack (1-2 hours before activity) in addition to your low-GI meal. A low-GI pre-workout snack will help to keep blood sugar levels stable, stave off hunger and ensure blood-glucose is easily available to the working muscles during your training or race.

Examples include:
- 1-2 bananas
- Sports or energy bar
- Cereal or breakfast bar
- Dried fruits such as raisins or apricots

FUELLING ON THE RUN

Unless you really are glutton for punishment, it's unlikely that your first obstacle race will encompass a full 24 hour 'Death Race' style event. If you're sensible, it's far more likely to be a race of somewhere between 10 and 15 kilometres and, as such, you will not really need to worry too much about eating during your training sessions or during the race itself. Of course, having said that, personal experience has shown me that having friends and family on the sidelines, armed with jelly babies, can work wonders to lift your spirits and energy levels.

VITAL FLUIDS

Your fluid intake is the most important thing to consider whilst you are training. Indeed, a loss of only 2% of your body's water content can lead to a dip of 10% in your performance. Dehydration will also make you more susceptible to cramps, nausea and reduce your ability to concentrate – not something that will aid your progress on a balance beam!

Whilst you are training make sure you take water with you, and drink it little and often, rather than gulping down huge amounts when you are thirsty.

Top Tip: If you are not a fan of water, or find it hard to drink, why not make your own isotonic sports drink by mixing equal parts of fruit juice and water and adding half a teaspoon of salt (optional).

On race day water consumption may be harder; some races will have water stations whereas others (ones which are based in forested or harder to access areas) may not. When they do, use them, a swig of water will make you feel much better throughout the duration of your race.

If you know that your race does not have water stations along its route then don't panic. Make sure that in the days leading up to your race you stay well hydrated and sip an isotonic drink little and often on race day in the hours before you set off.

POST-RACE REFUELLING

Although the first thing you may want to reach for once you've crossed the finish line is a nice cold beer, it will, sadly, not be the best choice to replace the fluid, glucose and electrolytes you will have lost during the race. Rehydrate yourself following the guidelines below, then go off and celebrate!

Fluids

As an experiment you could try weighing yourself before and after a hard workout session (where you have sweated lots) and record how much weight you have lost. Any resulting weight loss will be mainly due to the loss of fluid through sweat. For example, a loss of 0.5kg equates to a loss of 500ml of fluid.

As you will continue to sweat for a while after exercise and your body will require fluids to begin repairing and restoring itself, you should aim to drink a bit more fluid than you have lost. For example, if indeed you have lost 0.5kg you should try to drink 750ml of water (little and often) to replace the fluid. Again, if you do not like water on its own, treat yourself to a homemade isotonic drink instead.

Food

You should try to consume something within two hours of training or racing which, if you're anything like me, won't be hard as I'm always ravenous after a workout or race!

This time, however, opt for a meal that is of moderate- to high-GI foods so that your body can get the glucose into the bloodstream that it needs to replenish the depleted stores in your muscles. Also, add a source of protein to the snack or meal so your body can use this to begin repairing any damaged muscle tissue.

Examples:

- Dried fruits and nuts
- Porridge made with milk and honey or jam
- Sandwich/wrap/bagel with cottage cheese or tuna
- Rice cakes with jam or peanut butter

Don't worry if you don't feel like you can handle solid foods after training or immediately after racing, try some of these liquid substitutes:

- Fresh fruit smoothie, get creative with your flavours and add some yoghurt or milk
- Flavoured milk or homemade milkshake
- Meal replacement (carb/protein) shake

Central YMCA Health and Fitness Guides

4

WEAR IT WITH PRIDE

When it comes to deciding what to wear on race day, there really is only one thing to remember: **comfort**. Obstacle racing is physically and mentally challenging enough, the last thing you need is to be worried about your top riding up, leggings riding down or shoes giving you blisters.

WICKING WAYS

When buying kit invest in modern 'wicking' fabric, which moves moisture away from the body towards the outside of the material where it can evaporate.

Training benefits:
- Increased comfort as sweat will be moved away from the body faster
- Protection against the cold

Racing benefits:
- Protection from the cold: moisture from various water obstacles will not cling to the body and make you colder
- Extra protection against obstacles

The kit you race in should be the kit you train in – **don't try anything new on race day**. Try different combinations of kit while you are training, and put your kit through the same demands as it will face on race day to see which pieces work best for you.

When you are choosing your kit be mindful of the demands that will be placed on you on race day. Will the course be muddy? Will it be rocky? Will it be dusty? Will it be hot, cold, raining or snowing?

Here are some considerations for each of the pieces of kit you may (or may not) wear.

TOPS

Long-sleeve vs. short-sleeve?
This comes down to personal preference and the race conditions. During the obstacle race you will be crawling through mud and stones, under cargo nets, scaling and swinging over man-made wooden and metal structures and charging through water. Long-sleeves will help protect your forearms from sharp stones or edges and will provide an extra bit of warmth if you are racing in the cold. However, if you are lucky enough to be racing in warmer conditions, you may find that the extra layer leaves you hot and uncomfortable. The best advice is to try both of them whilst you train and see which is the best for you. Don't be afraid to try a combination of the two!

BOTTOMS

Shorts vs. Tights?
The great thing about running tights is that they will offer your legs more protection than shorts while you are charging through water crossings or careering through some heavy undergrowth. They will also provide that extra layer if you are racing out in the cold. If, however, you are racing in the warmer months or warmer parts of the world you may find that wearing tights will make you uncomfortably hot.

Even if you are racing in the cold remember that because your leg muscles will be doing most of the work, they will heat up and retain that heat. This inevitably means that even though you may be cold when you set out, you will warm up quickly and may find you are too hot with your tights on.

Before you make your decision, consider when and where the race will be, how comfortable each option was during your training and how happy, or not, you will be with having some war wounds at the end of the race.

FANCY DRESS?

I have seen it, but never done it. Wearing fancy dress may be quite a novel idea, it may increase your sponsorship fund if you are running for charity and, depending on the outfit, it may also provide some amusing photos. However, remember that you will receive none of the benefits of the technical fabrics in terms of protection or warmth and you may find (depending on how ridiculous the costume is) that it will hamper your race by getting stuck in or on some of the obstacles. Bear safety in mind too: you don't want the tail of your monkey costume to get caught at the top of a giant wall, leaving you hanging precariously in mid-air.

FEET

There is an amazing array of shoes on the market for 'off-road' running, 'cross-training' and fell running, each with clever sole design, tread pattern and motion control. While these technically advanced, top of the range shoes may be impressive, you do need to consider where and when you will be running before opening your wallet. Bear the following in mind:

- If you're running in mud and ice through the winter, traditional trainers may not cut the mustard. You'll probably find yourself unable to get into any kind of rhythm around the course due to a complete lack of grip, ending up covered in more mud than expected.
- Equally, if you are running on hard-packed, dry, dusty and rock strewn terrain, wearing shoes with lots of soft rubber lugs (grips/treads which protrude from the sole) is not a good idea. They'll be so worn down by the end of the race that you'll need a new pair.

Here's my lowdown of what type of shoe you could use and when. Use this information as a guide; put the shoes you own through similar conditions to the ones you will be racing in and wear what works for you.

Trainers/runners

Trainers/runners would be the obvious choice and if you only have to buy one pair of 'exercise' shoes it tends to be this type. Trainers will work for most races. They are best placed for races in dry conditions, e.g. urban obstacle races, or races on dry, rocky or dusty terrain. Typically, you will be best off finding a 'cross-training' shoe as these will usually have more grip than a pure running shoe.

You can use trainers in muddier races but, as mentioned already, consider the fact that you may spend more time horizontal than vertical! If you are going to be running on a very muddy course you will be prone to slipping more frequently and you may find it harder to tackle certain obstacles, e.g. getting up steep muddy slopes (a favourite of some obstacle races).

Spikes

Spikes are a very specific shoe used by cross-country runners for races in foul conditions – think football boots with sharp spikes instead of studs. These are fantastic for grip, but are very dangerous in an obstacle race – imagine boosting someone over a giant wall and receiving a set of spikes through your hands as a thank you! For this reason races tend to ban the use of this type of shoe.

Trail shoes

If your race is going to be run entirely off-road and in muddy conditions then trail shoes should make things easier for you. These shoes have lugs on the bottom of the shoe that are specifically designed to give you more grip in muddy conditions. They also have stiffer soles which will protect your feet from impact on rocks or roots.

Lug length and pattern varies greatly from make to make, but for your first race I would opt for a pair with shallow, wide spaced lugs. Wide spaced lugs will allow mud to release easier while the shallower lugs will make them more versatile for other races.

Barefoot/minimalist shoes

Barefoot running is growing in popularity and using this style of shoe will offer you benefits to your running form, stride efficiency and running economy. However, be prepared for a long transition between standard running trainers and minimalist footwear. You will need to allow sufficient time for training and for the adaptation of the small muscles in your feet and calves as these would not have been relied on as heavily when you were running in standard trainers. For starters, scale back any distance running and limit yourself to just 10% of what you were doing, gradually building up by 10% each week.

If this is a route you would like to explore, remember that taking your shoes off or buying minimalist shoes will not automatically make you a good barefoot runner. Also, be sure you are comfortable with this type of footwear on the terrain you will be racing before you reach the start line!

SPARE CLOTHES

Spare clothes on race day are always part of my essential kit as I have always got soaked to the skin or covered in mud in every race I've ever taken part. For this reason my spare clothes include a number of t-shirts and jumpers to layer up, fleece-lined trousers and fresh underwear! If your race is in drier (not muddy) conditions, spare clothes may not be essential. However, travelling home in sweaty kit is never a pleasant experience, especially if you have other people with you.

Also, remember that you will need a spare pair of shoes if you don't want to be treading mud/dust etc. into your or your friends' cars!

Central YMCA Health and Fitness Guides

5

WORKING UP A SWEAT

When finding an area in which to train it is best to replicate the kind of conditions you will be racing in, as specificity in your training is the best way to prepare mentally and physically for the race. Here are some potential areas you could train in with some considerations for each:

GYM OR STUDIO

OK, so you won't be completing an obstacle race in a gym or a studio, but both do have their uses in terms of finding suitable places to train.

Training in gyms and studios with weights and cardiovascular equipment offers a measurable way of training, e.g. you can monitor your speed on the treadmill and write down what weights you are lifting. By keeping a log of these you will be able to see how you are progressing.

You may also find that some gyms have functional training equipment such as suspension training kits, climbing frames and monkey bars. These are all perfect training for obstacle races as they are more specific than standard, fixed-resistance machines.

All of the circuits that are listed in the *Zero to hero in 12 weeks* training plan can be replicated in a gym or a studio. However, do make sure you abide by the rules of the gym. Remember that not all kit is there to be used as a climbing frame or balance beam.

PARKS

Training outdoors offers more specificity than training indoors as you will be running on surfaces similar to your race and all the exercises you will be doing will be based around pushing, pulling and otherwise moving your own body weight without the support of machines in the gym.

In short, parks are great places to train and boast a wealth of space and landmarks that you can build into a training session. Here are some examples:

- Benches to jump onto
- Walls or frames to climb over
- Big slopes to sprint up
- Trees to sprint between
- Posts to crawl between

Top Tip: Why not use the landmarks in your park, along with the exercises in the *Know your enemy* chapter, to set small challenges and even create your own personal obstacle race.

TRIM TRAILS

Trim trails are a fantastic place to train for obstacle races because they closely mimic race conditions. Trim trails are outdoor bodyweight circuit stations spaced out over an area (usually around a park) and linked by a running route. Typical stations will include pull-up bars, balance/parallel bars (for dips or inverted rows and hurdles), all of which are great exercises for conquering the obstacles in your race.

Top Tip: Find your nearest trim trail and experiment with the stations, try all the exercises and try using the stations in different ways; jump over them, climb them or crawl under them. You could even add in your own stations from the workout cards or exercises in the *Know your enemy* chapter. Both the 'sport specific runs' and the 'circuit' sessions in the *Zero to hero in 12 weeks* training plan can be completed on almost all trim trails.

6

KNOW YOUR ENEMY

Obstacle races, as their name suggests, have a vast and varied array of obstacles for you to climb over, jump through and crawl around, with each race also inevitably boasting a signature obstacle to add a little extra spice.

What follows is a list of the most common obstacles in their most basic forms. You will, however, undoubtedly come up against obstacles that have not been specifically mentioned below as each race will adapt obstacles or put two or more together to make hybrid, super-obstacles! Nevertheless, using the list and exercises below will at least allow you to understand what you are up against and offer you some tips to tackle them.

1. **The hay bale(s)**
    What is it?
    Hay bales are a favourite in obstacle races; used to create single hurdles to jump over or mighty pyramids that have to be scaled before you launch yourself down the other side. Climbing over these is surprisingly taxing as it is a whole body, strength-based action.
    Conquer it
    The best training for these is to embrace your inner child and get climbing! During your runs get used to jumping onto something and pulling yourself over the top – walls, climbing frames or pull-

up bars.

Also do

Burpees or squat jumps to improve your vertical leap, parallel bar/bench dips, push-ups, pull-ups or inverted rows to build strength in the upper body (chest, back and arms) to haul yourself over the obstacle.

2. The giant wall

What is it?

Sooner or later you'll hit The Wall; not the metaphorical version that marathon runners talk about, but an altogether more tangible Giant Wall…and it may not be limited to one per race. Walls can come in a variety of shapes and sizes; some will be A-frame shape, whereas others will take a traditional vertical wall. Each can range in size from 2 to 3 metres (7 to 10 feet). Some walls will have tools in place to help you clamber up – such as beams, foot holds or ropes – whereas for others you'll simply need a big jump (or a boost from another competitor), coupled with lots of upper body strength to haul yourself over.

Conquer it

Preparation for these is similar to hay bales, get out there and get climbing!

Also do

Squat jumps focusing on height will improve your vertical leap. Pull-ups and press-ups for upper body strength to pull yourself up and over the wall.

3. The fire pit

What is it?

Fire pits are dug around half a metre deep and half a metre wide, filled with hay and slow burning fuel. In the interest of safety fire pits will usually follow a water obstacle or water crossing to make sure you are soaked before jumping through the flames. They can also be a welcome sight if you are freezing cold from the last few water obstacles. Flame height will vary from race to race, but they will seldom be above knee height.

Conquer it

Jumping through fire will require a speedy run up and a good single footed jump. Practise taking a short sharp run up then exploding off one foot, propelling yourself forward to cover as much ground as possible.

Also do

Sprints; sprint for 20 seconds, rest for 10 seconds, repeat 4 times, rest for 2 minutes. Two footed and single leg broad jumps.

4. **The commando crawl**

   What is it?

   Commando crawls are the same in every race. While the surface and the material you are crawling under may well change, you are still essentially down in the dirt crawling along on your belly. If you are crawling under netting, keep your head down and your shoulders and hips up to create the room to crawl through. A bit of etiquette here, once you are clear of the netting hold the end up for the next person coming through. Girls, make sure your head is down and your hair is tied up tight, lots of hairbands get lost in the netting. If you are crawling under barbed wire – keep everything as low to the ground as possible, there will be sufficient room to crawl under, just make sure you don't get caught. If you are crawling through tubes – go towards the light!

   Conquer it

   While you are running practise your crawling technique – crawl between goal posts on a (vacant) football pitch, crawl under (vacant) park benches. Practise crawling up and down hills if the opportunity presents itself – not all commando crawls will be on a flat surface.

   Also do

   Spiderman push-ups; bring one knee towards the same elbow as you lower yourself to the ground. Walking plank; from a push-up position, move one arm at a time to come to rest on your forearm, and then back up to rest on your hands.

5. **The balance beam**

   What is it?

   Not as physically demanding as other obstacles, but a real challenge nevertheless. If you are already tired, wet, cold, or if they are covered in mud, balance beams can be as hard to overcome as any of the other obstacles. Balance beams can be very low to the ground, where it really doesn't matter if you fall off, or they could be six metres (20 feet) above land where falling off will see you plunging into safety nets or water! Unsurprisingly, they can therefore be more psychologically challenging than physically challenging.

Conquer it

Practise balancing along a wall or a see-saw. Practise balancing during the rest part of your runs; this will allow you to get your breath back while challenging your mental fitness and balance. Above all, however, be safe!

Also do

Single leg balances; try moving your other leg around to increase the stability challenge.

Single leg squats; with the non-squatted leg unsupported.

Single leg deadlifts; start un-weighted and gradually add weight

6. **The water crossing**

What is it?

Water crossings can vary in length, from a simple chest high trench to an imposing river that you'll have to swim across and, depending on the running conditions, they can be good or bad news. If, for example, you are running in blazing heat then they will provide some welcome refreshment. However, if you are racing in cold conditions then water crossings can come as a huge shock to the system. In these conditions my advice is to keep your eyes fixed on the person in front of you and match them step for step, or stroke for stroke, until you are out the other side.

Conquer it

Unless you are sure of the streams or rivers around you wild water crossings are unadvisable due to undercurrents. Always put your safety first. Instead, you can run or wade through the shallow end of a swimming pool to get used to the drag of the water.

Also do

Step-ups with a knee raise onto a low wall or bench. Lunges and sprints will build strength in the lower body to charge through the water.

7. **The monkey bars**

What are they?

Monkey bars are another obstacle race classic and they'll usually be positioned over something you don't want to fall into (mud, water etc.). This obstacle is all about upper body strength and timing your swings between the bars.

Conquer them

Trim trails and or play grounds will have monkey bars for you to practise on.

Also do

Pull-ups, to build upper body and grip strength.

8. **The big hill**

What is it?

Obstacle races inevitably include big hills as a way to tire out your legs and leave you gasping for air. Some hills will be short enough to sprint up, others will have you grinding to a crawl using the roots and trees to help pull yourself up to the summit. Some slopes may even be so steep and muddy that ropes will be anchored at the top to allow you to drag yourself up. Traction on these steep muddy slopes is near impossible, so lean back as you climb up the rope to help you reach the top.

Conquer it

Find a short, steep hill near you (something that takes up to 30 seconds to sprint to the top) and sprint up it. Find a safe way down, use this as your rest, and repeat 4-8 times.

Also do

Rope pull get-ups; anchor a piece of rope over a frame or pull-up bar, lie on your back holding the rope and use your upper body only to pull yourself up to a standing position.

9. **The mud pit**

What is it?

Knee-deep sloshy mud that acts like quick sand, once your feet sink in it'll take a lot to get them out. The best way to tackle these kinds of obstacles is to hit them at speed as, by being quick and light on your feet, you won't sink so far into the mud. Another tip: look at the rest of the people in the pit and pick the route that has the fewest racers struggling knee deep in mud!

Conquer it

Sprints; 20 second sprint, 10 second rest, repeat x 4. Try some on a flat and some up short hills.

Also do

Step-ups with knee drive on a low wall or bench, if you do get stuck in the mud this will give you lower body strength to get out.

10. **The tyre dash**

What is it?

A long stretch of old tyres laid flat in front you. The tyres will be a deliberate mixture of heights and sizes, from car to tractor, to try and throw you off your rhythm. My advice: pay attention to where you put your feet, make sure they go right in the centre of the tyres and take shorter steps to avoid tripping over. Concentrate on picking your knees up high to be sure your feet are clear of the tyres.

Conquer it

30 metre stretches of tyres are hard to come by so, instead, do high knee drills between sets of trees focusing on having light feet and picking your knees up.

Also do

Multi-directional lunges to get used to changing direction whilst still maintaining balance.

Less common obstacles and how to deal with them

1. **Electric wire**

What is it?

Sometimes known as jelly-fish tentacles; strips of live electrified wire hung from frames that you either have to run or crawl through. This is not a pleasant experience and can, literally, be quite a shock to the system.

Conquer it

There is no real way of preparing for these, just get through them as quick as you can! With some races boasting live wires pumping out as much as 10,000 volts you don't want to be hanging around when it comes to this obstacle.

In my experience you have two options: 1) try to sneak your way through the wires without touching any of them or 2) barrel through them at a sprint – either way you are unlikely to miss being zapped. Go with which ever methods feels right on the day, my main tip for these is to keep your face covered with your arms as you go through.

2. **Mental challenges**

   What are they?

   In very rare cases races will require you to complete a mental challenge; this might include a memory or logic task or a puzzle of some description.

   Conquer them

   Even though you are tired you will still need a sharp and focused mind for these tasks. Try to build them into your training as much as you can – write small logic puzzles on cue cards and add the puzzles in as additional stations to your 'sport specific runs'. The internet is a great source of puzzles should you require them.

3. **Gauntlet**

   What is it?

   British Bulldog for adults! Essentially, you will have to run between two points whilst two or more people (usually in fancy dress and armed with padded sticks) try to hinder your progress by pummelling you.

   Conquer it

   For this one you will need to be quick on your feet and able to change direction at high speed to dodge, duck and dive your way through the gauntlet. Do deceleration training; sprint for 5-10 seconds, decelerate as fast (hard) as you can and change direction (lateral/side step) and continue to sprint for another 5 seconds. Rest and repeat.

Central YMCA Health and Fitness Guides

7

RACE TACTICS

Are you running on your own or in a group? Is your event a mass start or are you running in waves? If you are running in waves then which one should you pick? What will happen if you are faster than all your friends? What happens if you are injured and cannot complete?

The first two questions you should be able to answer straight away and, by the end of this chapter, you should be able to answer the others, too.

RUNNING SOLO

Running solo can be an invigorating and liberating experience. It's just you versus the obstacles, and the clock. Racing on your own allows you to run your race the way you want to; you can put the hammer down when you are feeling good, put the brakes on when you are struggling and hit obstacles with as much (or as little) vim and vigour as you can muster.

It is worth noting, however, that although invigorating, running solo can be hard for motivation. Fellow competitors in most races will spur you on – especially if you pick someone in front of you to try and catch – but on occasion you may find that you're a long way away from other competitors, or just plain exhausted, at which point loneliness can kick in and motivation, along with performance, could drop significantly.

Top Tip: Prepare for this by trying longer, 'sport specific runs' on your own to get used to the feeling of pushing yourself while you are on your own. It can help to have a time in mind if you are running solo as this will give you something to focus on through some of the tougher parts of the race.

RUNNING IN A GROUP

Running as a group (two or more) is a great experience; you and your friends versus anything the race can throw at you.

Running in a group means that you can spur each other on when the going gets tough, help each other over obstacles, share the enjoyment of the experience and celebrate the achievement with a group of mates.

If you are running as a group it is a good idea to attempt a few group runs in training; you could try some of the 'sport specific' sessions as a group. This will give you all a gauge of each other's fitness levels, as well as the individual strengths and weaknesses that you can then look to support over the course of the race.

So, what happens if you are faster than all your friends when it comes to race day? This question needs an answer before you get to the start line, as it'll be difficult to answer during the race, especially if there are only two of you! Decide as a group (before you set off) whether you are going to stick together (no matter what), or split up if some of you are faster.

MASS START EVENTS VS. RUNNING IN WAVES

Mass starts are inevitably exciting, but will only happen during small events for obvious safety reasons. As their name suggests, every single competitor will line up behind the start line and charge off at the sound of the claxon.

If your race is a mass start event then be prepared for the initial charge away from the line and lots of jostling for position in the early stages. The best option for mass start events (unless you are trying to break the course record) is to let everyone tear off at break-neck speed, just settle into your own rhythm and pass them all a few kilometres into the course when they've exhausted themselves!

Waved starts are favoured when races have large numbers of competitors. Waves will, at most, be made up of 250 people who will set off at approximately 30 minute intervals. If you are lucky enough to be able to choose which wave you run in, think about what you want to achieve from the race. If you are aiming for a specific time, consider running in the first 2-4 waves (the first wave will usually be full of athletes looking to break course records). By setting off in these waves the course ground will be relatively undisturbed – making muddy courses or sections easier and ensuring there is not as much bunching or hold-ups on the obstacles.

If you book a race at the last minute, or you have no control over what wave you run in, you might find yourself running in a much later wave. By starting later you may encounter the following (these are not meant to put you off, just to prepare you):

| | **Bunching on obstacles**
Bottle necking is common with some of the harder obstacles or obstacles where only a set number of people can pass through at any one time (e.g. very steep hills, banks or tunnels which you have to crawl through) so be prepared to be slowed down by this throughout the race. It is unlikely to happen throughout the whole race, in most races you may find pockets of space where you can traverse the distance and the obstacles with relatively little bunching.

| | **Course conditions**
Having somewhere between 250 and 2,500+ competitors bare down on an already muddy or dusty course will make it harder. The ground will be churned up either filling the air with dust or making the whole course a mud-skating rink. Obstacles will be harder to negotiate, especially if they have been made slippery by being covered in mud.

If you are running in either a mass start or waved event, make sure you know your specific start time and that you arrive at the race with plenty of time spare for your own peace of mind.

DNF

The dreaded DNF (did not finish). These are three letters that no competitor wants to have next to their name on the final race listings. DNFs can be hard to take; lots of competitors would rather walk, crawl or drag their way around a course instead of not finishing. However, DNFs are not something to be feared, and many top athletes such as Peter Reid (world class Ironman triathlete), Mara Yamauchi and Ryan Hall (2012 Olympic marathon runners) have DNFs next to their names. There is absolutely nothing wrong with being taken out of a race or taking yourself out of a race if you are injured or physically incapable of completing. Lining the sides of races are stewards, first aiders and paramedics, all there for your safety. In some of the more gruelling races it is not uncommon to see paramedics pulling competitors out of the race because they are turning blue or otherwise unable to continue racing. By listening to the medical professionals and your own judgement a DNF one day means that there will be a next time. If you chose to disregard the medical advice or your body's screams on race day, your injuries may mean that mean finishing this race could be your last.

8

FAIL TO PREPARE, PREPARE TO FAIL

Race day is looming, your excitement levels are growing, as are your nerves. Don't worry, everyone else will be feeling the same way. This chapter focuses on all the logistics you will need to consider before the race, so that you can dispel the nerves and enjoy race day itself.

THE NIGHT BEFORE

The night before your race is the perfect opportunity to make all the preparations necessary to ensure that your race day is smooth and stress free. Preparing everything the night before will also be good psychological preparation for the race which can help to ease those last minute nerves.

If the organisers sent you a race pack, take some time to look through the contents:

  - Fill in all the information on the reverse of your race number and make sure you have safety pins to attach it. (In some cases you will be collecting your race number on the day.)
  - Attach your timing chip to your laces. I made the mistake of not doing this once and ended up losing it somewhere in a hotel room!
  - Look over a map of the area or a list of some of the obstacles, if one has been provided. Take some time to reflect on all the

amazing training you have been doing specifically for all these tasks and how much fun you are going to have conquering all of them!

☐ Lay out all your kit; race kit in one pile, spare clothes packed up in your rucksack or in another pile ready to pack.

A general checklist follows, which will hold true for most races, however you may receive special instructions which will be communicated to you via email or in your race pack, so make sure you pay attention to them.

OBSTACLE RACE CHECKLIST

Make sure you have all these things packed and in place ideally the night before your big day:

☐ Directions to the race and a generous estimated time of arrival for transfer time from your home or hotel to the site

☐ Racing kit (you may be wearing this on the way to the race)

☐ Race number: Make sure you fill in all the details on the back and you know your official start time (you will have to collect these at registration on the day for some races)

☐ Timing chip: Attach this to the laces of your shoes the night before

☐ Spare clothes: You will probably want a whole new set of clothes (yes, that means underwear too!)

☐ Spare shoes

☐ Towel

☐ Plastic bags: For wet and muddy kit

☐ Parking pass (if required)

☐ Bottle of water or isotonic drink

☐ Food for the finish line: Something delicious, you've earned it.

☐ Friends to cheer you on!

9

RACE DAY

PRE-FLIGHT CHECKS

On the day itself make sure you arrive in plenty of time. I arrived so late to one race that I had to sprint from the car park to the start line as my wave was setting off – not the best warm up!

Race day proceedings will vary from race to race and you may have to collect a race number or timing chip on the day, which will be made clear on your confirmation emails. Factor in some queuing time if this is the case.

Some races require you to attend a safety briefing before you start; this will be a 15-20 minute talk about the course conditions, including any last minute changes and the safety issues presented by obstacles you will come up against. Do attend these and do pay attention, they contain vital information and are for your safety.

You will be required to sign a disclaimer; the disclaimer (or 'Death Warrant' as its referred to in the Tough Guy race) will state that the very nature of the event you are entering is dangerous and that you should not only be in good physical condition, but that you are aware of the inherent risks of participating in such an event. The disclaimer will go on to say that you are solely responsible for your actions and any resulting injuries, thus waiving your rights to claim compensation. You should be 100% certain that you are happy to sign the disclaimer before signing it, so do it read it carefully,

Central YMCA Health and Fitness Guides

then read it again, before putting pen to paper.

PRE-RACE WARM UPS

Warming up thoroughly will help you prepare physically and mentally for the race, so do give yourself an opportunity to warm up properly. Performing a warm up will prepare your muscles, heart and lungs for what is ahead, which can minimise your risk of injury. Your warm up should include actions that mimic the movements you will be doing throughout the race – this is known as 'skill rehearsal' or a 'sport specific' warm up.

Skill rehearsal during your warm up is very important, as it allows the neuromuscular pathways between your brain and muscles to warm up in preparation for coordinating whole body movements such as jumping, crawling and climbing. This type of warm up has been shown in some studies to offer a performance boost, as well as injury prevention (*http://www.sciencedirect.com/science/article/pii/S1440244008000790 / ymcaed.org.uk/ip*).

Some races will offer an instructor-led, group warm up, details of which are given on the day. They will usually take place at the start line, just before the claxon. If your race does not include a warm up (you will find this out on the day) use the RAMP-ing up warm up in the *Zero to hero in 12 weeks* training plan that follows.

THE START LINE: 10 SECONDS TO GO

Acknowledge your fellow competitors and those friends you have roped into running with you, shake their hands, give them a high five and get ready. The noise level will start to increase, with whoops, shouts and cheers, so immerse yourself in the noise of the crowd and the other competitors on the start line. Join in the count down:

10…9…8…(butterflies should be kicking in)…7…6…5…(heart may be in your mouth!)…4…3…(gulp) 2…(don't worry, you've got this – get out there and have some fun!) 1…GO!!!

POST-RACE DAMAGE CONTROL

CONGRATULATIONS. You've run, jumped, crawled and climbed around the race and crossed the finishing line, no doubt, with your hands in

50

the air like a superstar! And rightly so, you've earned that finishing line! Well done!

Depending on how hard the course was (and how hard you raced it) you may not want to think about anything other than celebrating once you have crossed the finishing line. However, here are some things that are really worth doing before you get too carried away with celebrations:

- Collect your medal and goodie bag
- Give back your timing chip – there's normally a big bucket to throw them in
- Cool down and stretch; this may be the last thing on your mind, but performing one of the cool downs in my training plan will help to bring your heart rate back down to normal, flush out any residual lactic acid in the muscles and should help prevent some of the muscular discomfort you are likely to feel tomorrow
- OK. Now off you go – get changed and get celebrating!

Central YMCA Health and Fitness Guides

10

ZERO TO HERO IN 12 WEEKS TRAINING PLAN

This plan is designed to take you from the sofa to the finish line of your first 10km obstacle race. The weeks are broken up into five sections, each of which is detailed below.

The programme combines long, slow distance sessions to target the cardiovascular system, with circuit-based sessions to mimic the movements and demands placed on the body during an obstacle race.

Most of the exercises are straightforward and well known; they can all be found on popular video sharing websites, together with examples of progressions if you feel you are not being challenged enough.

For those exercises that you might not be able to find online I have attempted to explain and break them down as part of the workouts that follow.

If your fitness level is already high make some of the following changes:

- choose exercise progressions to a make the sessions harder
- repeat the circuits for more rounds
- decrease the rest time between exercises

For the monitoring of the intensity of the sessions I have used the adapted 1-10 Borg Rate of Perceived Exertion Scale (Borg et al. 1983) (a category-ratio perceived exertion scale: relationship to blood and muscle lactates and heart rate).

12-week overview

Weeks 1-4: Base fitness phase with two days' rest between sessions

Frequency: 2 sessions per week
Intensity:
Session 1: RPE 5-7
Session 2: RPE 6-8
Time:
Session 1: 30-40 mins
Session 2: 30 mins
Type:
Session 1: Long, slow distance (LSD) training
Session 2: Circuit session - *First base* (weeks 1 & 2); *Second base* (weeks 2 & 4)

Weeks 5-6 : Power phase with at least two days' rest between the circuit and sport specific run

Frequency: 3 sessions per week
Intensity:
Session 1: RPE 5-7
Session 2: RPE 6-8
Session 3: RPE 6-8
Time:
Session 1: 40-45 mins
Session 2: 30 mins
Session 3: 30 mins
Type:
Session 1: LSD training
Session 2: Circuit session: *Power to the people*
Session 3: Sport specific run: *3, 2, 1 + 1 DASH!*

Weeks 7-8: Speed phase with at least two days' rest between the circuit and sport specific run

Frequency: 3 sessions per week
Intensity:

Session 1: RPE 5-7
Session 2: RPE 6-8
Session 3: RPE 6-8
Time:
Session 1: 40-50 mins
Session 2: 30 mins
Session 3: 30 mins
Type:
Session 1: LSD training
Session 2: Circuit session – *AMRAP*
Session 3: Sport specific run – *L'addition s'il vous plaît*

Weeks 9-11: Sport specific phase with at least one day's rest between each sport specific run

Frequency: 3 sessions per week
Intensity:
Session 1: RPE 5-7
Session 2: RPE 5-9
Session 3: RPE 5-9
Time:
Session 1: 50-65 mins
Session 2: 30 mins
Session 3: 30 mins
Type:
Session 1: LSD training
Session 2: Sport specific run – *Play your cards right*
Session 3: Sport specific run – *Play your cards right*

Week 12: Taper with at least two days' complete rest before race day

Frequency: 2 sessions per week
Intensity:
Session 1: RPE 5-7
Time:
Session 1: 30 mins
Type:
Session 1: Sport specific run – *Taper tantrum*
Session 2: Sport specific run – *Taper trail*

12 week specifics

Week 1:

LSD session
- ☐ Always use *LSD1 warm up* for LSD sessions
- ☐ Target time for the main section is 10 minutes. Try to jog as much as you can, when you need to rest to catch your breath slow to a brisk walk. When you have caught your breath bring your pace back to a gentle jog. Repeat this sequence until you have reached 10 minutes, then go into *LSD cool down*.

Circuit session
- ☐ Perform *First base* workout

Week 2:
LSD session
- ☐ Increase the time of the main workout to 15 mins

Circuit session
- ☐ Perform *First base* workout

Week 3:
LSD session
- ☐ Increase the time of the main workout to 20 mins

Circuit session
- ☐ Perform *Second base* workout

Week 4:
LSD session
- ☐ Same as Week 1

Circuit session
- ☐ Perform *Second base* workout

Week 5:
LSD session
- ☐ Increase the time of the main workout to 20 mins

Circuit session:
- ☐ Perform *Power to the people* workout

Sport specific run:
- ☐ Perform *3, 2, 1, + 1 DASH!* workout

Week 6:
LSD session
- ☐ Increase the time of the main work out to 25 mins

Circuit session:
- ☐ Perform *Power to the people* workout

Sport specific run:
- Perform *3, 2, 1, + 1 DASH!* workout

Week 7
LSD session
- Increase the time of the main work out to 30 mins

Circuit session:
- Perform *AMRAP* workout

Sport specific run:
- Perform *L'addition s'il vous plait* workout

Week 8
LSD session
- Increase the time of the main work out to 30 mins

Circuit session:
- Perform *AMRAP* workout

Sport specific run:
- Perform *L'addition s'il vous plait* workout

Week 9
LSD session
- Increase the time of the main work out to 35 mins

Sport specific run:
- Perform *Play your cards right* workout twice this week

Week 10
LSD session
- Increase the time of the main work out to 40 mins

Sport specific run
- Perform *Play your cards right* workout twice this week

Week 11
LSD session
- Increase the time of the main work out to 45 mins

Sport specific run
- Perform *Play your cards right* workout twice this week

Week 12
Sport specific run
- Perform *Taper tantrum* workout card

Central YMCA Health and Fitness Guides

- Perform *Taper trail* workout card

The warm ups and cool downs

1. LSD warm up

- 2-3 minutes brisk walking
- Walking step-throughs: lift one knee up so that your thigh is parallel to the floor; extend the knee to feel a stretch through the back of your leg (hamstring); place the leg down and repeat x 10 on each leg
- 30 seconds brisk walking
- Walking high knees with side squat: perform three steps bringing your knee as high as you can, on the third step hold the leg in the air, take a large lateral step and squat down. Repeat x 5 on each leg
- 30 seconds brisk walking
- Walking step-backs: the reverse of walking step-throughs. With the knee up high, push the leg behind you as you step back
- 30 seconds power walking
- Rotational reach squat: squat down, touch the outside of one foot, as you stand up reach up high through the opposite shoulder. Repeat this x 5 on each side
- Power walk to jog strides: over 10 steps increase your speed from a power walk to a jog; jog for 3-4 steps and return to a power walk. Repeat 7-10 times.
- Begin your run!

2. Cool down – LSD cool down

- 30 second to one minute power walk, slowing to one minute brisk walk
- Rotational reach squat
- 30 seconds brisk walk
- Walking high knees with side squat, x 5 each leg
- Walking step-throughs x 10 each leg
- Walking step-backs x 10 each leg
- Walking triceps stretch (arm above head)
- Walking shoulder stretch (arm across body)
- Static stretches for calves, hamstrings, quadriceps, glutes and inner thigh

3. Warm up – First base

- 2-3 minutes brisk walking
- Dynamic chest stretch: start with arms in front of you, palms together. Step forward with one leg into a shallow lunge, pull the arms apart until you feel a stretch across the chest. Repeat x 10 changing legs each time and opening the arms in different directions
- Dynamic flexor chain stretch: start with your arms extended in front of you, step back into a shallow lunge, lean back slightly as you reach behind you. Let your eyes follow your hands. Repeat x 10
- 30 seconds brisk walk
- Rotational reach squat, x 5 on each side
- 30 seconds power walk
- 30 seconds power walking, every 10 steps perform three (unloaded) thrusters; squat down and, as you stand up, perform a shoulder press (push your arms up over your head)
- Power walk to a nearby tree, perform 10 easy push ups with hands against the tree
- Power walk to a nearby tree, flex at the hips, place your hands on the tree, lean into the tree and bend the elbows taking the crown of your head to the trunk. Extend the arms pushing your head away from the tree (keeping your hips flexed). Repeat 10 times

4. Cool down – First base

- 30 second power walk
- Rotational reach squats, x 5 on each side
- 30 seconds brisk walk
- Dynamic chest stretch x 10
- Dynamic flexor chain stretch x 10
- Walking triceps stretch (arm above head)
- Walking shoulder stretch (arm across body)
- Static stretches for calves, hamstrings, quadriceps, glutes and inner thigh

5. Warm up – RAMP-ing up (raise, activate, mobilise, potentiate)

- 2-3 minutes brisk walking
- Dynamic chest stretch x 10
- Dynamic flexor chain stretch x 10

- Walking step-throughs x 10 each leg
- 30 seconds brisk walking
- Walking high knees with side squat x 5 each leg
- 30 seconds brisk walking
- Walking step-backs x 10 each leg
- Rotational reach squat x 5 on each side
- 30 second power walking, every 10 steps perform three (unloaded) thrusters
- Power walk → jog strides: over 10 steps increase your speed from a power walk to a jog, jog for 3-4 steps and return to a power walk, perform one Inch Worm (start in Downward Dog, walk out hands into or just past push up position, walk feet in to meet hands). Repeat x 5
- Jog → ¾ pace sprint: over 10 steps increase your speed from a jog to a ¾ pace sprint, carry this speed for 5-8 steps and return to a jog, perform one (shallow) Dive Bomber. Repeat x 5

6. Cool Down – RAMP-ing down

- One minute jog
- One minute power walk
- Walking high knees with side squat x 5 each leg
- Walking step-throughs x 10 each leg
- Walking step-backs x 10 each leg
- Dynamic chest stretch x 10
- Dynamic flexor chain stretch x 10
- Walking triceps stretch (arm above head)
- Walking shoulder stretch (arm across body)
- Static stretches for calves, hamstrings, quadriceps, glutes and inner thigh

11

THE WORKOUTS

Workout name:
First base
Equipment:
Pull-up bar or bar for inverted rows (e.g. inverted 'U' to lock a bike to)
Low wall or bench for step-ups
Warm up:
First base warm up
Main workout:
Complete each exercise for 30 seconds, rest only as long as it takes to get into position for the next exercise.
NOTE: Be strict with these rest periods, it should only be just enough time to get into position for the next exercise.
First round:
1. Pull-ups/jump pull-ups (if you can't lift your body off the floor do a small jump to help) or inverted rows (if no pull-up bar)
2. Walking plank: Start in a push-up position, lift one arm and place the forearm on the floor, repeat with the other arm. Now reverse this, lift one arm, place hand on the floor, repeat with other arm.
3. Squats: To make these harder you can try adding a calf raise or squatting on one leg.
4. Gracie drill: Start in push-up position, lift one arm off the floor, step the opposite leg through, return to a push-up position. Repeat on the other side.
5. Push-ups.

6. Walking lunges.
7. Mountain climbers.

One minute rest: Use this to grab a drink and do some balance drills. Standing on one leg, walking along a wall or straight line etc.

Second round:
1. Pull-ups/jump pull-ups or inverted rows
2. Walking plank
3. Step ups with opposite knee drive – use a step, bench or wall
4. Gracie drill
5. Walking lunges
6. Dive bomber push-ups
7. Mountain climbers

Optional: Depending on your fitness level you may feel the need to complete one or both of these rounds more than once each.

Cool down
First base cool down

Workout Name:
Second base
Equipment:
Pull-up bar or inverted row bar
Low wall or bench for step-ups
Warm up:
First base warm up
Main workout:
Complete the two exercises back to back, 30 seconds each. Rest for 10-20 seconds. Move on to the next exercises.
Round one:
1. (1) Pull-up (or jump pull-up) or inverted rows + (2) back extensions
2. (1) Squat (make harder as per C1) + (2) step-ups with knee drive
3. (1) Walking plank + (2) Gracie drills
4. (1) Mountain climbers + (2) Lunges
5. (1) Loaded thrusters (use a log, rock or rucksack to add weight) + (2) Dive Bomber push-ups

One minute rest: Use this to grab a drink and do some balance drills. Try some single leg deadlifts (start un-weighted), walking along a beam or a wall etc.

Repeat for a minimum of two rounds in total

Optional: Depending on your fitness level you may feel the need to complete this more than twice. You also may wish to decrease the rest periods between exercises to make this more challenging.

Cool down:

First base cool down

Workout name:

3, 2, 1 + 1 DASH!

Equipment:

Pull-up bar or inverted row bar

Warm up:

RAMP-ing up

Main workout:

Perform:

1. 3 x broad jumps.
2. 2 x plyometric/clap push-up (if you cannot perform full clap push-ups, do them in a ¾ position or have your hands higher than your feet. The emphasis here is on explosive power).
3. 1 x pull-up (move to jump pull-ups or inverted rows if pull-ups become impossible).
4. Run for 2-3 minutes.

Perform the exercises again adding 1 repetition to each exercise. Repeat until you are performing 7-10 repetitions of exercise 3.

Optional: Depending on your fitness level you may feel the need to complete this more than once or increase the maximum repetitions of exercise number 3 beyond 10.

Cool down:

RAMP-ing down

Workout Name:

Power to the people

Equipment:

Karate belt/yoga strap

Pull-up bar or inverted row bar

Warm up:

RAMP-ing up

Main workout:

Perform each exercise for 5 repetitions with 30 seconds rest between the exercises – make them hard enough that you feel you couldn't do a sixth repetition. Follow each exercise with an isometric hold (see below) for the same muscle group. Repeat these until you have completed 1-3 sets of each exercise.

Isometric holds

Isometric holds activate the nervous system to contract muscles maximally through (in this case) three stages of an exercise.

Example – Squat Isometric Hold

Stand on the karate belt, hold the bottom phase of a squat, hold the ends of the belt in your hands taking up all the slack. Hold on tight to the belt and drive up as if you were standing up (the tension on the belt will stop you doing this), contract the muscles as hard as you can for 10 seconds. Rest for 10 seconds, come to the mid-phase of the squat, take up the slack on the belt and try to stand up (contract maximally) against the resistance of the belt (remember the belt should hold you in a fixed position). Rest for 10 seconds, repeat at the top phase of the squat (just before full hip extension).

Exercises:

- Box jump (use a wall or bench)
  Isometric hold: Squat
- Plyo/clap push-up (concentrate on explosive reps, even if the push-up position needs to be regressed)
  Isometric hold: Standing chest press (wrap belt around tree)
- Plyo pull-up/inverted row: For this exercise focus on an explosive pulling phase, ripping your body away from the floor
  Isometric hold: Standing row (wrap belt around tree)
- Multi-direction shoulder throw – grab a rucksack (nothing breakable inside) or other weight, hold it to your chest. Explosively throw the bag/weight into the air as high as you can. Try throwing these in different directions – straight up, slightly forward, slightly to each side etc. (make sure you have enough space for this one!)
  Isometric hold: Standing shoulder press (stand on belt)

Optional: Depending on your fitness level, you may feel you need to repeat this circuit more than three times.

Cool down:
RAMP-ing down

Workout name:
L'addition s'il vous plait
Equipment:
None!
Warm up:
RAMP-ing up
Main workout:
Perform exercise 1, followed by a 2-3 minute run. Repeat exercise 1 and 'add-on' exercise 2, followed by a 2-3 minute run. Repeat this process until you have completed the last exercise.

Exercises:
1. High knees x 5 each leg
2. Commando crawl for five seconds, jump up and sprint for five seconds x 4
3. Power skips x 5 each leg – remember the playground skip when you were younger? It's like this but now you want to jump up as high as you can off each skip
4. Deceleration with direction change – sprint a short distance at top speed, decelerate as quickly as possible and change direction, e.g. shuffle laterally 3-4 steps x 10 (5 x left, 5 x right)

Optional: Depending on your fitness level this circuit can be completed more than once.

Cool down:
RAMP-ing down

Workout Name:
AMRAP

Equipment:
Karate belt/yoga strap

Warm up:
RAMP-ing up

Main workout:
This circuit is a circuit against the clock. You have 10 minutes to complete **A**s **M**any **R**ounds **A**s **P**ossible.

This work out only has one built-in rest period; if you need more rest, take it – just remember the premise of the circuit – As Many Rounds As Possible.

Complete as many rounds/reps as you can in 10 minutes:

Exercises:
1. 10 second sprint, 10 seconds rest x 4
2. Rope/belt stand-ups x 5: Wrap a yoga strap or karate belt around a pole or tree, lay on your back with your feet underneath where the belt is looped round and hold onto the ends of the belt. Using your arms (and lats) only, pull yourself up to standing and lower yourself back to the floor
3. Plyometric/clap push-ups: Concentrate on explosive push-ups (use a ¾ push up position or have your hands higher than your feet to make this easier) x 10
4. Mountain climbers x 10

Optional: Depending on fitness level you can increase the time of this circuit or complete it more than once.

Cool down:
RAMP-ing down

Workout Name:
Play your cards right
Equipment:
Deck of cards
Other specific equipment
Warm up:
RAMP-ing up
Main workout:
This is your chance to get creative! Take a deck of playing cards, pick four race specific exercises (from this programme or the *Know your enemy* chapter) and relate each to a different suit, e.g.

Hearts = Dive bombers
Diamonds = Rope stand-ups
Clubs = Commando crawl + sprint
Spades = Burpees

- Run for 2-5 minutes
- Stop, take out the deck of cards turn over the top card
- The suit will denote the exercise and the number will denote the repetitions
  Picture cards are as follows:
  Jacks – 11 reps; Queen – 12 reps; King – 13 reps; Ace – 14 reps; Joker – 20 reps of every exercise
- Complete between 3-6 cards per circuit
- Repeat for 30-60 minutes or until you've finished the deck

Cool down:
RAMP-ing down

Workout Name:
Taper tantrum
Equipment:
Pull-up or inverted row bar
Warm up:
RAMP-ing up
Main workout:
Perform exercise 1, followed by a 2-3 minute run. Repeat exercise 1 and 'add-on' exercise 2, followed by 2-3 minute run. Repeat this process until you have completed the last exercise.
Exercises:
1. Single leg squats x 5 each leg

2. Dive bombers x 5
3. Pull-ups x 5

Cool down:
RAMP-ing Down

Workout Name:
Taper trail
Equipment:
Karate belt/yoga strap/rope
Low wall or bench for step-ups
Warm up:
RAMP-ing up
Main workout:
Perform exercise 1, followed by a 2-3 minute run. Repeat exercise 1 and 'add-on' exercise 2, followed by 2-3 minute run. Repeat this process until you have completed the last exercise.
Exercises:
1. Step-ups x 5 each leg
2. Rope/belt stand-ups x 5
3. Push-ups, hands higher than feet x 5

Cool down:
RAMP-ing down

Central YMCA Health and Fitness Guides

12

RUNNING FOR CHARITY FAQ

Given the gruelling nature of obstacle racing, people often choose to participate to raise money for charity. This can take two forms. Firstly you may wish to purchase your place in the race, and then contact a charity to notify them of your intentions to run the race on their behalf. By doing this there will be no minimum sponsorship target. Or, secondly, charities may have places which they will allocate to competitors who agree to raise a minimum target. As this style of racing is becoming more popular and quickly becoming oversubscribed, charities have begun to advertise places to competitors who are willing to raise money for their charity. The London Marathon is a good example of such charity placement schemes. If you are going to race for charity here are some FAQs to get you started:

Q) How would you approach a charity to run in a race for them?
A) Charities' contact details can be found on their websites. Do contact them as they may be able to offer support and in some cases may be able to get local press coverage for you!

Q) Can you use the charity logo if you are running for them?
A) If you are taking a charity space then most charities will provide you with literature and even t-shirts to run in.

Q) If you are running for a charity, do you have to wear their logos or colours?
A) This is optional – it might raise more awareness but do remember the benefits which the more technical fabrics give you.

Q) Can you use online donation accounts (e.g. www.JustGiving.com), and is this organised by you or the charity?
A) You can, and are encouraged to use online donation accounts because they are easy to set up, easy for people to donate, and the link to your donor page is easily publicised. You will usually have to set these accounts up yourself.

Q) If there are more applicants than runners what are the criteria to be met in order to be chosen?
A) Some charities will ask you to complete an application form if you are taking a charity place. On this form you will need to detail why you want to raise money and awareness for that particular charity and how you are planning to raise money for them. Some charity application forms may even want you to show a breakdown of how you will reach your target sponsorship, such as setting projected sponsorship goals for the months leading up to the race.

Q) How long after the race is the payment expected?
A) Most charities expect 100% of the minimum sponsorship target to be sent to the charity six weeks after the event.

Q) What happens if a minimum sponsorship target is not reached?
A) Most charities (as mentioned above) will ask for projected sponsorship targets in the months leading up to the race and will have frequent email or telephone contact with you to check your progress. If you do not manage to reach you minimum sponsorship target some charities will allow a re-negotiation of deadlines for when the money has to be in, whilst others may decide to blacklist you from further events.

Run, jump, climb and crawl

If you are running for a charity create additional sponsorship events to help meet your fundraising target. Here are some ideas to whet your appetite...

- Car boot/yard sale
- Raffle
- Homemade cake sale
- Pub quiz
- Hair removal
- Bachelor/Bachelorette auction
- Ticketed event e.g. dinner or ball etc.

Well go on then, get on with it! That money won't raise itself.

Central YMCA Health and Fitness Guides

BIBLIOGRAPHY

Books

Bean, A. (2002) *Food For Fitness*. London: A&C Black Publishers Ltd.

Lawrence, D. and Hope, B. (2008) *Advanced Circuit Training*. London: A& C Black Publishers Ltd.

Fleck, S.J. and Kraemer, W.J. (2004) *Designing Resistance Training Programmes*. Champaign, IL: Human Kinetics

Hodge, K. (2005) *The Complete Guide to Sports Motivation*. London: A & C Black

Chu, D.A. (1998) *Jumping Into Plyometrics*. Champaign, IL: Human Kinetics.

Websites

www.pponline.co.uk/encyc/the-borg-scale-how-accurately-does-it-measure-an-athletes-training-intensity-106

www.sciencedirect.com/science/article/pii/S1440244008000790

www.bmi-calculator.net/bmr-calculator/bmr-formula.php

Central YMCA Health and Fitness Guides

www.bmi-calculator.net/bmr-calculator/harris-benedict-equation/

www.food.gov.uk

www.amazon.co.uk/Need-Guide-Nutrition-Exercise-ebook/dp/B00BFXT6DI

www.glycemicindex.com/index.php

Run, jump, climb and crawl

ALSO OUT NOW

If you enjoyed this book you may also be interested in reading:

20 full body training programmes for exercise lovers
By Darren O'Toole BSc

Available now on Amazon.com

www.ymcaed.org.uk/20FBT

Central YMCA Guides
Trustworthy advice from those in the know

Central YMCA Health and Fitness Guides

Run, jump, climb and crawl

THE CENTRAL YMCA GUIDE SERIES

Happy and Healthy: A collection of trustworthy advice on health, fitness and wellbeing topics

UK www.ymcaed.org.uk/hhct2
US www.ymcaed.org.uk/hhct

The Scientific Approach to Exercise for Fat Loss: How to get in shape and shed unwanted fat by using healthy and scientifically proven techniques

UK www.ymcaed.org.uk/sael2
US www.ymcaed.org.uk/sael

The Need to Know Guide to Nutrition for Exercise: How your food and drink can help you to achieve your workout goals

UK www.ymcaed.org.uk/ngne2
US www.ymcaed.org.uk/ngne

The Need to Know Guide to Nutrition and Healthy Eating: The perfect starter to eating well or how to eat the right foods, stay in shape and stick to a healthy diet

UK www.ymcaed.org.uk/gnhe2
US www.ymcaed.org.uk/gnhe

Central YMCA Health and Fitness Guides

Tri harder - the A to Z of triathlon for improvers: The triathlon competitors' guide to training and improving your running, cycling and swimming times

UK www.ymcaed.org.uk/thtc2
US www.ymcaed.org.uk/thtc

20 Full Body Training Programmes for Exercise Lovers: An essential guide to boosting your general fitness, strength, power and endurance

UK www.ymcaed.org.uk/tpel2
US www.ymcaed.org.uk/tpel

Gardening for Health: The Need to Know Guide to the Health Benefits of Horticulture

UK www.ymcaed.org.uk/gfhh2
US www.ymcaed.org.uk/gfhh

New Baby, New You: The Need to Know Guide to Postnatal Health and Happiness - How to return to exercise and get back in shape after giving birth

UK www.ymcaed.org.uk/nbny2
US www.ymcaed.org.uk/nbny

The Need to Know Guide to Life with a Toddler and a Newborn: How to prepare for and cope with the day to day challenge of raising two young children

UK www.ymcaed.org.uk/ngtn2
US www.ymcaed.org.uk/ngtn

Discover more books and ebooks of interest to you and find out about the range of work we do at the forefront of health, fitness and wellbeing.

www.ymcaed.org.uk

Made in the USA
Middletown, DE
11 December 2018